"Nicole is a master at breaking down the compo̶n̶e̶n̶t̶s̶ ̶o̶f̶ ̶t̶h̶e̶ ̶ podcasting into easily digestible tidbits that are relevant to those just starting their own show, all the way to podcast veterans. She's got a simple and direct delivery - and she dives deep into vital topics that every podcaster can learn something from. I highly recommend this book to all those interested in improving their shows." .

—Eric Kussin, SameHere Global Mental Health Movement, We're All A Little "Crazy"

"I read Nicole Christina's wonderful 'Not Just Chatting' from the point of view of an interviewee rather than a podcaster. Even from the 'opposite' standpoint, I learned so much that can shape my own lectures and presentations.

In 2019, I had the pleasure of being interviewed by Nicole for Zestful Aging. At that time, I was a podcast novice, this being only the second I had done, but found the experience both enjoyable and educational.

*'**Not Just Chatting**' is a quick and engaging read, and I came away with a new understanding of various listening and preparation techniques that can cross over into activities other than podcasting. For example, on how to create a clear vision of what you wish your audience to come away with, and the importance of quality rather than quantity in terms of both the number of podcasts (better to have a quality podcast bi-weekly than a mediocre one very week) and the timing of each one (30 minutes is an optimum sweet spot as it is the average time of a morning commute).*

Nicole does not hold back as to the dedication and time required to make each 30-minute interview meaningful for the audience, and helpfully guides the podcaster on how to avoid the process becoming repetitive and tedious, leading to the possibility of 'pod fade' setting in.

Nicole's own enthusiasm for her well-chosen interviewees is truly infectious, and as the recipient of her gently probing style (Nicole is *a practicing psychotherapist), I have no doubt about this. Her revelation that she is smiling when she is introducing her guests comes as a delightful image, but no great surprise. I would highly suggest that every potential and new podcaster casts their eye over '***Not Just Chatting***'. You will find it a wonderful and indispensable read."*

—Gillian Walnes Perry MBE, Founder, Anne Frank UK

Not Just Chatting

How to Become a Master Podcast Interviewer

Nicole Christina

DEDICATION

This book is dedicated to Steve, my stalwart supporter, without whom there would be no "Zestful Aging"; my dear friend Amy, the most devoted friend I could ask for; and Davis, whose spirit and sense of humor bring joy to me every day.

And to my podcast guests: thank you for sharing your stories with me. Your willingness to be open and honest has made me a better interviewer and has enriched my life immensely.

CONTENTS

INTRODUCTION

You might have noticed that everyone and their sister is podcasting. From the high school student next door to Ellen DeGeneres, podcasting is enjoying huge popularity. There are even jokes that "everyone has a podcast now." According to PodcastHosting. org, as of March 2021 there are 1,900,000 podcasts and over 47 million episodes. That's a lot of competition.

Some of the reasons for the dramatic increase in podcasts are obvious; it's fairly straightforward to start one, with even options that allow you to do it for free. YouTube offers many good tutorials. The idea you can have your own "channel" potentially heard by thousands, even millions, is very seductive. Podcasts are also being used as a way to increase revenue for businesses, especially entrepreneurs. They can be used as one facet in a marketing strategy to promote one's product. Podcast listeners tend to be affluent and educated, which makes them sought after customers. And during the global pandemic, people had more time to research and create their own show.

The simple truth, though, is that after you get over the thrill of being a podcaster, you realize there's a lot of competition for ears. It becomes painfully clear that people haven't been waiting for you to put up your first episode. The rate of attrition is significant, even having its own name: Podfade. Podfade is a real threat to your podcast career: according to PacificContent, 12% of podcasts have only published a single episode, 6% haven't made it past two episodes, and half of all podcasts have 14 or fewer episodes. So you need to do everything possible to avoid burning out.

You will be less likely to fall victim to podfade by having good, memorable interviews. Learning basic interviewing skills will help you stay invested in your show. Knowing how to conduct a good interview will help you enjoy your guests. Your guests are more likely to enjoy the interview as well, and that makes for a positive feedback loop. This enjoyment will come through. Your audience can hear it. And they will want to listen again. You will feel some success and that will help you do the required work. You'll be in it for the long game.

In this primer, we'll be focusing on upping your interview game—or at least putting interview skills on your radar. You might have assumed that interviewing a guest is just like chatting to a friend; they say something, and you say something, and on and on. It's a conversation. We have them all the time. Maybe you love to talk with people and are a gregarious person. And maybe you have some natural skills for listening and asking questions. But to get the most out of your guests, following some basic principles will result in a much better experience for your audience, your guests, and you. You want to rise above the many short-lived and mediocre shows, so you need to sound professional and know how to bring out the best in your guests. By best I mean bringing out the "good stuff"—the interesting tidbits that go beyond the usual vanilla questions and answers. Guests who are honest and real are so much more interesting than what you will typically hear. This is the special sauce that entices your audience and motivates them to share your podcast with their people.

One of the comments I get regularly from guests is how much they enjoyed our interview. I take pride in making it fun for them. Good interviews have a way of leaving both you and your guest energized, enriched, and feeling connected. Because we are mammals, we are hardwired to connect with one another. Your audience will benefit from that feeling of connection and want to hear more from you. They will want to get to know you. They will feel understood and included. You will be improving their lives, and doing your small part to improve the world. In that way, podcasting offers many of us a sense of purpose and meaning. Finding purpose in life is one of the proven ways to age well. In my case, this is practicing what I preach on *Zestful Aging*.

I've been a psychotherapist for almost 30 years, so I've earned my stripes as an interviewer. Interviewing well is a vital part of being a good therapist as well as being a good podcast host. Looking for themes, listening deeply, and knowing when to be silent are just a few of the skills I've honed by speaking with thousands of clients. It's a skill that can be learned, but it takes practice. I think you'll find learning these skills fun, because you will see instant results. And you'll develop confidence as a podcast host that will come through in your interviews. You'll feel more calm and in charge. You'll have a general plan but also be flexible enough to go in another direction with your guest to get to the good stuff. And the more you feel comfortable with your skills as an interviewer, the more you will be able to enjoy the conversation. In that way, all of the behind-the-scenes work podcasting requires will be worth every minute.

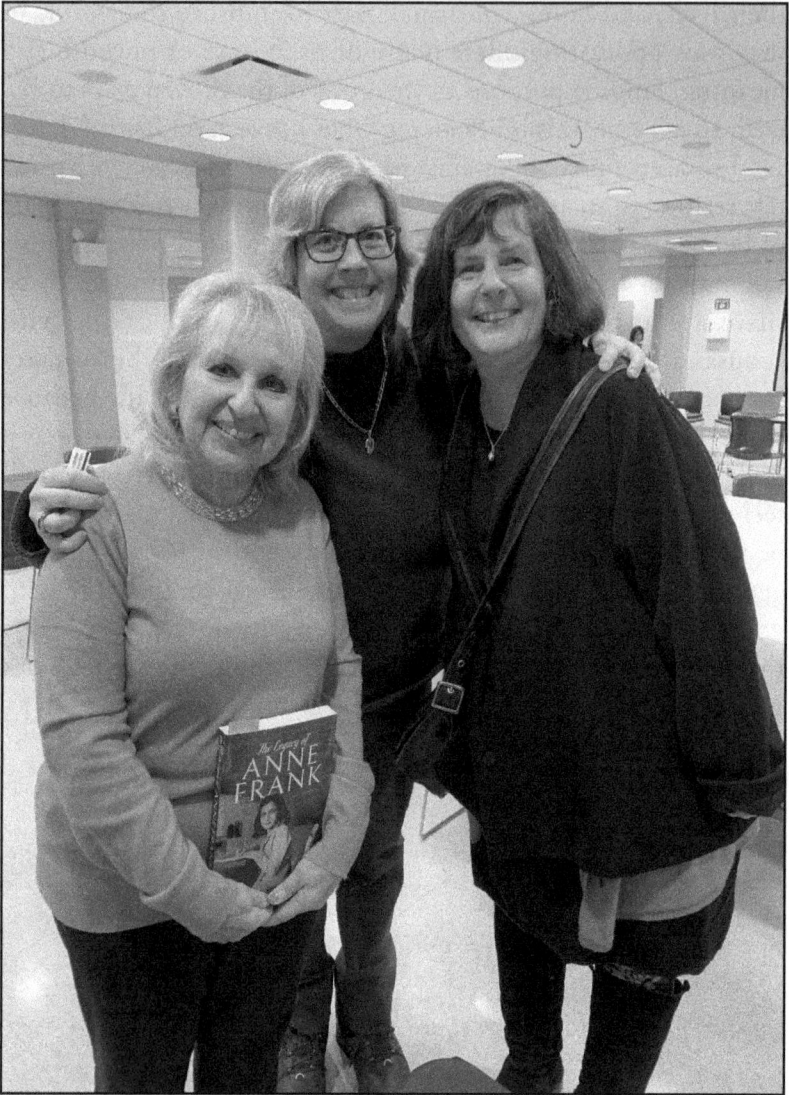

Zestful Aging Podcast guests from two continents meet: L to R: Gillian Walnes Perry (UK), Diane Weiner (Syracuse University) and author meet at Syracuse University.

CHAPTER 1
PODCASTING IS LIFE CHANGING

Being a podcaster offers you a platform to share yourself and your interests and meet people from all over the world, even some you might have to locate on a map! And it's fun to be known as a podcaster. It's a little taste of celebrity. It's been life changing for me, and interviewing my inspiring guests has allowed me to maintain hope even as the world faces severe challenges. Interviewing guests who are doing good in the world leaves me inspired and moved. One such example is actor Sandy Fish who played the evil mother in the Netflix cult series "Sense8." She spends much of her free time at San Quentin Prison teaching prisoners to care for fellow prisoners in compassionate caregiving at the end of life. My life has been enriched by speaking to her and learning about her dedication to these marginalized men. Or Barbara Demorest of "Knitted Knockers" who organized a group of breast cancer survivors to travel to Africa to teach other survivors how to knit their own breast prosthetics—without sharing a common language.

Podcasters like to call their show their "baby," and it's not surprising. Podcasts are a lot of work, and we put our whole selves into them. To further the metaphor, they are a labor of love, often passion projects, to which we are deeply attached. We love our own podcasts. We take pride in them. I could talk about *Zestful Aging* for hours. It's a reflection of what I find important and interesting in the world. Podcast interviews have a more personal feel than many other types of interviews. They can feel more intimate than a typical radio interview. Terry Gross of *Fresh Air* is known for her ability to have candid conversations with her guests, but she's always representing NPR. If you are an independent podcaster, as I am, you have total freedom to interview anyone you want and to ask them what you want to ask. You, and only you, are accountable to your audience. That's both a freedom and a responsibility. And often you are doing your own production work. The scheduling, the editing, and the promoting are often done by the host. It truly is our work.

Podcasting gives you a new identity. When people ask me what I do, I say I'm a "professional podcaster and a psychotherapist." I started adding "professional" recently not only because I make money through sponsorships, but because I want to bring a feel of professionalism to it. Anyone can be a podcaster, but it takes skill and practice to become a pro. I'm proud of the work I've put into my show to improve and refine it over the years, and you will be too as your podcast evolves. I've listened to my earlier interviews, and I've definitely developed an ease and spontaneity over time. Hosting a podcast gives you admission to an exclusive club. The popular *She Podcasts* has a very active Facebook group, where the administrators clearly state that if you are not a podcaster, "this club is not for you." Podcasting groups have subgroups, based on topics, like True Crime. And there are many podcasting conferences all over the world springing up every day. It's become a subculture all its own. Podcasting offers you a tribe of new people who understand the unique experience you share. A sense of belonging is very beneficial to your life and health—it's how humans are wired.

Even when we are not interviewing, serious podcasters are thinking about their ideal future guests. I watch TV with an eye on who would make a great guest. Once I was watching a documentary about wastewater from mining operations polluting native lands in the Southwest. The professor being interviewed was a tribal leader dedicating her life to stopping this harmful practice. While I was watching the show, I found her on Twitter and asked her to be on my show. She accepted before the show was over! One evening after randomly catching her show, I was also thrilled to book popular PBS travel host Samantha Brown after admiring her approach to travel and her cultural humility. Recently, I contacted a Facebook friend that I didn't know directly but had published a book that caught my eye. Judging from her profile and interests, she just seemed like someone I wanted to connect with. I invited her to meet virtually to talk about our common interests. We had a lively, long ZOOM meeting discovering other commonalities and I scheduled an interview on the spot! Whenever I see vibrant looking women, either on TV or social media, I wonder if they would be great guests. It's a fun challenge to see if they accept my invitation.

I like to be prepared for the possibility of meeting a potential listener or guest on any given day. I carry business cards with my podcast logo and my contact information. I even have some in my tennis bag and car. You never know when you will have the opportunity to talk to someone who might be interested in listening. It also further demonstrates you are a professional and that your podcast is not a fly-by-night operation.

Being a part of the podcasting world opens you up to new experiences. Learning new things is energizing and helps us age well. It wouldn't be an exaggeration to say podcasting has given my life more meaning and a sense of belonging to a group of interesting and passionate (mostly) women. I feel a sisterhood with many of my guests, some of whom I stay connected with long after our interview. Last winter, I had the chance to meet Gillian Walnes Perry, the co-founder of Anne Frank UK, when she came to the U.S. to give a talk about her book on Anne Frank. I had connected her with professor and poet Diane Weiner, another guest, from Syracuse University who I knew had an interest in diversity and inclusion. Diane invited Gillian to speak at Syracuse University about her book and her life advocating for peace and justice. It was definitely a "pinch me" moment (see photo).

Another guest, Antonia Rolls, also from the UK, painted a picture of me using a photo I sent her, to include in her art exhibit on families of addicts. We plan to meet next Thanksgiving when she travels to the US. Through a set of strange circumstances, I ended up knitting a hat for actor Sandy Fish for her trips to San Quentin Prison. She posted herself on social media wearing the hat I made her. Being a podcaster offers you membership into a new world—one of shared interests and passions. It opens the door to meaningful connections that are sometimes surprising, and often wonderful. And there is no end to the number of guests out there waiting to meet you through your podcast.

It's also been quite a thrill to speak with guests who are influencers. Some of my guests have been interviewed by Terry Gross on *Fresh Air*. In fact, I interviewed Peggy Orenstein the day after she was on *Fresh Air*! Speaking with guests like Joan Lunden is like having a backstage pass to the work of culture changers. It's a real thrill. Another satisfying aspect of podcasting is connecting guests with one another. I love to offer connections that might be helpful or just fun for my guests. And I've found that guests are likely to reciprocate. There's a feeling of sharing the love among podcasters.

Many of my guests are writers. In order to prepare for our conversation, I almost always read their books. When I set up the interview with my guest, I ask if they would mind sending me a copy of their book. To date I haven't been turned down. A large majority of the guests inscribe their books, so I have a keepsake of their episode. I have a bookshelf in my living room of all of my guests' books. It's a source of pride and sentimentality for me. And a few times I've even had the book in my collection before it's been published. Another benefit of interviewing interesting and accomplished guests is that you learn more about the world. I've become better read and more interesting as a result of speaking with my guests and reading their books.

Your podcast is a direct expression of who you are and what is important to you. You are revealing yourself to your audience on many levels. They learn what you value, what interests you, and who you are. As a podcaster, you are putting yourself out there for the world to see—and judge. It's a vulnerable position, and it takes some courage. But if you don't let your audience know who you are, they are not going to connect with you as a host. You need to be a real person, even at the risk of being criticized (one review on iTunes described my voice as too annoying to listen to). You are having a kind of intimate relationship with your listeners. Your listeners will expect certain things from you. You become a virtual friend of sorts. They may be interested in your guests, but you are the constant presence and that can be comforting—especially in today's world. They can count on your episodes being aired at predictable times. Don't underestimate how important that can be.

Even the decision on how to order your episodes needs to be done intentionally. I try to balance lighter subjects with more serious subjects, like facing mortality. At one point so many guests were talking about death and dying that I quipped I should rename my podcast "Deathful Aging." Give some thought to how you want to order your shows and what content works best for particular seasons, holidays and current events. I decided to pull an episode that was about chair yoga the week George Floyd was killed. It felt insensitive to run an episode that was cheerful and bouncy when the world was grieving.

If you have sponsors, they may have the power to make decisions about the content of your show. For most of us, every decision is ours. That's both the good news and the bad news. It's scary to make choices that may end badly. Also, you may experience decision fatigue if you are a solo podcaster and need to make every single decision related to your show. But I find it energizing to find guests who will be perfect for my audience, and make a new connection that may bear fruit later on. That's part of the fun.

Zestful Aging listeners know I value resilience and courage in the face of aging. They expect some levity, even during interviews covering difficult subjects. And they know that it's not unusual for my guests to become emotional because we're often talking about serious challenges they've experienced or important problems in the world.

After a particularly engaging interview, it takes me a little while to come down emotionally from the experience. It's so intensely satisfying that I might even be a little tearful. I still can't believe I get to speak with culture changers from all over the world who have shared themselves so openly with me. I get to ask experts in their fields about things about which I am genuinely curious. Recently, I interviewed renowned UK food writer Gilly Smith. She had just interviewed Ira Glass, the legendary host of *This American Life*. He's a podcasting icon. Before we even started talking about her interest in food production and the environment, we shared our deep admiration for Ira. One might even describe our chat as giddy!

Being a podcaster changes your life. It allows you access to people all over the world whom you'll never meet. You never know who's listening, and who will benefit from your inspiring interview with a well-chosen guest.

CHAPTER 2
WHAT'S YOUR VISION?

I was at the Apple store recently buying a new phone and spending what seemed like the entire afternoon with a salesperson. He was a friendly college student who was helping me transfer my data to the new phone. When he learned I was a podcaster he exclaimed, "That's so cool! I really want to be a podcaster!" When I asked him what he wanted to podcast about he said, "I really don't know."

Your podcast is the medium you use to send out your message. It's not an end in itself. Although it's a lot of fun, that will fizzle out quickly if you don't have a clear direction. Clarifying your "why," as has been said many times, is vital in producing a quality show. You may refine your focus as time goes on, but you must start with a clear idea of why it should exist in the first place. You need a well thought out plan, which includes identifying your audience and thinking about what your podcast offers to listeners. Otherwise it's just chatting into a mic.

A good podcast has a point and benefits your listeners in some way—and leaves them wanting to hear more. It offers a kind of community that resonates deeply with your listeners. The more specific your niche is, the wisdom is, the more likely you will be successful. It might seem like a good idea to try to cast a wide net and make yourself as popular to the mainstream as possible, but the opposite is true if you want loyal listeners. You want to give your audience something they can't get anywhere else. Your show will not appeal to everyone. In fact, the niche-ier, the better. To use an ice cream analogy, think in terms of espresso fudge swirl rather than plain vanilla.

My niche focuses on helping people reconsider their dread of aging by presenting many positive examples of people thriving after middle age. My listeners know I am a social worker, and my guests contribute to the common good. They aren't expecting political satire or a murder mystery when they tune in. My stated mission is to discuss what contributes to aging zestfully with expert guests and to have my listeners consider the power of leaving a legacy.

In order to get clear on your focus, consider these questions:

- What's the point of my podcast?

- Who is my audience?

- How will it benefit my listeners?

- What unique angle do I have?

- How can I make it stand out?

- Who are the guests that best fit my podcast's mission?

- What subjects excite me?

When I began, I decided *Zestful Aging* guests needed to be middle aged or older and female, but I soon realized there were some younger people who had interesting and helpful things to say about aging well. I was able to be flexible and broaden my vision for the podcast. You will evolve with your show. With my new guest guidelines in mind, I invited Sanjeev Javia, a young male entrepreneur, to be a guest. He knows a lot about the benefits of CBD, especially for active people. I thought he would be a great guest for my progressive audience, so I revised my original rule about my guests' age and gender. My focus is still on aging well, but with experience I learned that all of my guests don't have to be women "of a certain age" to be consistent with the theme of aging zestfully.

Your vision also needs to include presenting yourself as a professional in every aspect of your show's production and promotion. Make sure your logo and communications are well crafted. Think carefully when you comment on social media. Is that comment consistent with the image you want to project? Communicating with guests and sponsors needs to be done in a way that reflects well on you and your podcast brand. Use a spellchecker if you need to, but pay attention to the details. People form an idea about you and your show very quickly, and thus you want to do everything you can to appear polished and solidify that first impression. Do your research about what logos look best, or hire a professional designer to help. Fiverr is a good source for hiring out projects like this. Keep it simple and remember you are going to use your podcast name and logo for a long time to come.

Quality matters to your listeners. They want to be associated with something that's good. It says something about who they are as people. Think of it like a brand they want to identify with or a restaurant they frequent. How do they see themselves? How would they like to see themselves? My listeners are mostly middle aged and over women who are educated, progressive, and like interviews that go deeper and touch on emotional subjects, such as the ambivalence of caring for our elders and anticipating our own deaths. I call them the "NPR" audience. These folks are not going to be interested in potty humor or a focus on how to look younger. They are looking for a show that isn't mainstream and that is more cerebral. It's my job to be consistent, provide what I advertise, and respect my audience by doing everything I can to produce a quality show. Keeping your audience foremost in mind is a great approach to making decisions about your show.

Your vision for your show needs to be realistic. It's important to realize podcasting is a long game and requires patience. Have you heard the quip, "It took me 10 years to become an overnight success"? Unless you have a huge budget and can hire advertising experts, you can expect slow, but steady, growth. Checking your download stats can be fun, and even addicting, but they can be misleading. Stats don't show that the person is actually listening. Most experts suggest you pay attention to quality and the rest will fall into place. And sometimes it's hard to understand why one episode does well, while the next one falls flat. It bears repeating: Patience is a podcaster's best friend.

Chapter 3
CHOOSING YOUR GUESTS

Your choice of guests says everything about you and your show. This may be an obvious point, but it can't be overstated: It's of utmost importance that you choose your guests wisely, even (and maybe especially) when you are first starting out. When I first started podcasting, one of my early guests who gave me a great interview suggested I interview her best friend, a life coach. She sang her friend's praises. I agreed to have a pre-interview conversation with her on the phone. I'm glad I did. There were many buzzwords, but little content. I tried really hard to find something to grab on to, because I didn't want to disappoint my original guest. As I didn't hear anything that would contribute to my show, it was incredibly awkward. I had to tell her that I didn't think it would be a good fit. It was my introduction to one of the less enjoyable parts of being a host. I never imagined that I would have to veto potential guests!

Another time a podcast's agent, who are becoming increasingly popular, approached me. This particular one was working on behalf of his client who was an accomplished writer on a very popular subject. She had won awards. She was very complimentary about my Podcast. I was flattered. Her agent was persistent. The end result was a terrible interview in which, at one point, she asked me *my* opinion on her subject of expertise and I was caught totally off guard. Her agent contacted me when they hadn't heard from me, asking when the episode was dropping. I felt conflicted, obsessing about it for days. On the one hand, I told myself it wasn't *that* bad. But I had promised myself I would never compromise on quality. Finally, I decided to put the interview out at a time when I didn't think there would be many listeners, and I didn't promote it. I learned my lesson, though. Quality control is of the utmost importance.

It's uncomfortable to tell someone that they would not be a suitable guest, but your podcast is a total reflection of you. That's the beauty of it. I once saw a podcaster's conference presentation slide that said, "It's my Podcast and I can do whatever the hell I want with it." Don't let feeling awkward cause you to make decisions that might jeopardize its quality. At some point, you are going to have to turn guests away. It's best to do this politely, but clearly. Remember—there are two million podcasts out there. One bad episode may turn a potential listener away forever.

It doesn't take long until you are going to be solicited by agents whose job it is to get their clients interviews, especially if their book was just published. Agents can do a simple search of keywords on LinkedIn to find you and they can be downright pesky. You may receive several emails: "When can we set up an interview?" Don't forget that they are getting paid to get their client on as many podcasts as possible. They have their own agenda. It's not your job to help them book guest spots for their client. You don't have time to go into a long spiel about why their client isn't a good fit for you. You can write and save a reply in your documents for this occasion. A polite and concise email response might look like this:

> Thank you so much for your interest in the Zestful Aging Podcast. Unfortunately, your particular topic is not a good fit for *Zestful Aging* at this time.
> Best of luck,

Another possibility might be:

Thank you so much for reaching out. I am not scheduling any new interviews right now, but please feel free to contact me in late winter, etc.

I used to get really irritated when I sent out a query and heard nothing back. I swore I wouldn't be one of those inconsiderate people who did not respond to emails. But recently I got a guest request by someone who does mold remediation! I decided not to respond, because it was clear that they had not taken the time to see if their topic was a good fit with *Zestful Aging*. I also have made it clear I am not a fan of diets. When I'm not podcasting, I'm an eating disorder specialist, so I'm very wary and sensitive about attempts at weight loss. It's irritating to get queries from people who say their guest is a perfect fit—but who practice weight loss diets. Take an agent's recommendation with a grain of salt, and do your own research to see if their client is a great fit as your guest.

Choosing good guests naturally depends on the mission of your podcast. I enjoy a great deal of latitude in choosing guests, because everyone is aging. When I started, I focused only on guests who were women in middle age or beyond because I thought that reflected my audience. But after looking at the analytics, I was shocked to find that some of my listeners are not yet middle aged—and some are in their early 20's! It seems a good number of my listeners see the show as more aspirational, perhaps asking themselves questions such as "How do I eventually want to age?" "What can I do now to invest in my health and well being later on?" "How can I help my aging parents?" So the podcast's mission has changed a bit since I interpreted the analytics. Now I showcase guests who are involved in interesting and unique projects, but they are not all related to aging, per se. It also still has a humanitarian theme. I've highlighted the role of leaving a legacy, which further distinguishes me from the many other podcasts related to aging. You will refine your show as you gain more experience and get feedback from your audience.

I've also decided to include some male guests who have made significant contributions and whose work interests me. One example is Dr. Michael Fossel who is confident he is close to discovering the cure for Alzheimers. I would have been silly not to allow him to speak to my audience because he is a man. As your show evolves, you will tweak it to respond to your audience. As you evolve, your show will too.

At some point in the life of your podcast, you will be tempted to have a guest you feel lukewarm about, but he or she may be very persistent. *Don't do it.* It only takes one bad episode to turn off your audience. And they probably won't come back. Remember, your audience can choose from two million podcasts. Be super selective, and make sure your guests have something to offer your audience. A 15 minute phone chat can give you all the information you need. Are they engaging? Inspiring? Funny? Would you want to hear them talk about themselves and their project? Do you have a good initial rapport?

It's easy to be seduced by a potential guest's credentials. Once I had an impressive and accomplished guest who was involved in unusual, fascinating work. I was very excited to have her on my show. I was surprised when her delivery was monotone, which made for a pretty bland interview. Even though her work was groundbreaking, and even dangerous, her delivery made me want to take a nap. I made the newbie mistake of assuming she was going to be animated because of the kind of work she does. It bears repeating: Do your research.

I've heard other podcasters warn about inviting authors, in particular, without meeting them first in a pre-interview. It seems sometimes people who are expert writers aren't always so great at being interviewed. You need to screen your guests to make sure they aren't only working on interesting projects but are actually interesting to listen to. They need to be "good talkers"--energetic, interesting and enthusiastic.

You might also find your guest is a professional guest; that is, they have been interviewed many, many times. Those interviews may sound quite canned. Some guests have rehearsed their responses so many times that there's nothing spontaneous or natural about their delivery. If you can't get them to be more spontaneous in a pre-interview, you should pass, even if they are well known.

The best guests are the ones about whom you are curious. Only invite guests who *you* are excited to interview. Your enthusiasm and curiosity will come through, and that's what grabs your listeners. I can't tell you how many times people say to me, "I can hear the passion in your voice!" I don't have to pretend—I really am curious about my guests, because I pick ones I like. There's a world of interesting people out there. Don't pick a guest just because you think you should. It's your podcast, your perspective, and your personal work of art. Your choice of guests is a direct reflection of your values. That being said, less than one percent of my guests have been problematic. The overwhelming majority have been amazing, and some have even left me in tears.

Facebook and LinkedIn are good places to find guests, since these platforms determine your interests and show you things you've already shown interest in. I don't relish spending time scrolling through my Facebook feed, but some of the articles I find are goldmines for the kind of people I love to have on the show. People post articles on interesting subjects or they post articles they have written. From there, I google the author's name and see if I can contact them through Twitter, Facebook, or their website. Sometimes it takes some sleuthing if they don't have a presence on social media, but you can often leave a message on their company's website. I always describe the show, mention it's audio only, and that it only takes 30 minutes of their time. And I make sure they know what I specifically like about their work. This is really important. To break through the noise, they have to feel you are interested in them personally. I try to add something that connects us. And I try not to take it personally if they don't respond.

It helps to have thick skin when you ask people to guest on your show. I've invited guests on my show that I have no business asking. No, not Oprah. But other big people in the aging space.

But guess what? Some have said yes. It really helps if you can say "so and so recommended you" in the subject line of the email. If they just put out a book or a film, they want to promote it. It's free for them, and I only ask for 30 minutes of their time. I only record the audio, so that makes it even less burdensome. My email or tweet to them explains specifically why my audience would love to hear from them. This may be an obvious point, but do not use an email template. When I get solicited and the email begins, "Dear, Zestful," clearly it's a mass email—and a real turn-off.

Sometimes, try as you might, you can't convince people to be guests. I've heard that persistence pays off, but in my experience that only goes so far. I would love to interview Jane Goodall, for example. I love primates, and I've always deeply admired her. I contacted her agent and did about everything I could think of to convince her to agree. When the assistant told me Jane travelled a lot and was extremely busy, I even suggested interviewing her when she was waiting at the airport for her flight. Unfortunately, it wasn't enough. Many other culture influencers have agreed to be on my show, and I remind myself of the successes I've had. Ironically, I've had some big names agree to guest, while some lesser known people have turned me down or never followed up. It's hard to predict who will agree. Best not to take it too personally.

Once a guest agrees to be on your show, make it easy for them to schedule the interview. People really appreciate this. I recently got an email from a recent guest saying, "thank you for making the process so simple." Be flexible and respect their time. Be appreciative and gracious. Make sure your signature line has the icon of your show, as well as links to your podcast and social media. They may not have the time to be a guest, but they may want to hear your podcast. Don't miss a perfect opportunity to advertise your show.

One of my best tricks to get great guests is to get a referral from another guest. At the end of each interview I almost always ask, "Is there anyone you know who would be a great guest?" Then when you contact them, you say "So and so said you'd be a great guest." I've had a lot of success with this approach. And don't forget that people are busy. If there's someone I really want on my show, and they haven't replied, I'll follow up in a few weeks. I'm always surprised how overwhelmed people are. More often than not, they forgot to reply.

Choosing great guests is easier when you have a clear idea of what you are trying to accomplish with your show. Think about who your audience is and what they would likely find interesting. You can look at which episodes are your most popular to give you some ideas. My listeners are from all parts of the world, so I try to bring on guests that can speak about universal issues. It's important to me to connect with people from different cultures and be inclusive in general. I'm always on the lookout for a different perspective on aging. It's also more interesting for me. Remember, just because you interview someone doesn't commit you to airing the episode. If you don't think the show reflects well on you and your podcast for any reason, don't feel pressure to run it. It's better to have a quality broadcast bi-weekly than a mediocre one every week. Choose guests who have something to say and say it well.

My podcast guests' book collection. Most are autographed. It's grown two-fold since this photo!

CHAPTER 4
PREPARATION

Many people don't realize the work involved in producing one podcast episode, and succumb to "podfade"—they start out gangbusters and grossly underestimate the amount of labor necessary to produce one episode. The behind-the-scenes work is not always fun. Belonging to a community of other podcasters can be helpful in offering one another support. Search Facebook groups under "podcasting" and you will find many that are active and welcoming. Sometimes the work can be isolating, and a group offers a place to vent your frustrations and celebrate your download milestones. I've also found some great guests through these kinds of groups.

The interview itself is actually a small fraction of the total work involved. Believe it or not, it's at least 4 hours of work to get a 30 minute episode ready to drop. There's the work of finding the guest, scheduling the guest, a pre-interview if necessary, recording the episode, editing, and publishing. Not to mention advertising and posting on social media. You have to love your podcast to work on it for little or no pay, at least starting out. It requires discipline to meet your deadline every week. Most experts agree that consistency is extremely important, and there will be times when producing your episode feels more like a grind than an inspired work of art. Some of these jobs can be outsourced, and I recommend that, but prepping for the actual interview is not one of them. It's almost impossible to do all of the tasks by yourself, unless you don't have a job, a family, or anything else to do with your time. Asking for tech assistance in podcasting groups can be a good way to get the help you need. As podcasting has become more popular, a whole industry is developing around supporting the podcaster and the related tasks.

If you are tempted to skip preparing for your interview, don't. It's the foundation upon which the whole interview rests. Think about it like painting a room; sure, you can open the can and get right to it. But painting tape and a drop cloth go a long way in making the job more professional and higher quality. Do your research. Knowing some quirky details about your guest's life provide the little gems that make for a great interview. Intimate details or funny little stories make your podcast stand out. Your guests will also feel respected that you bothered to research them. In fact, they will like you for it. Yes, it's time consuming. You may think you want to be "spontaneous" in your interviews. But knowing about your guests' backstories will give you confidence because you already have a sense of who they are. You will know what kinds of questions bring out the best in them and get them really engaged—and you will make an actual emotional connection. Your audience will feel it. These details will bring a whole new depth to your conversation and prevent it from sounding like a bunch of superficial soundbites. You want your interview to be rich and unique. That's how you set yourself apart from a very crowded playing field.

Here's an example of how a small detail made for a much better interview: I recently interviewed Jo Moseley, a woman in the UK who paddleboarded across the UK alone, *picking up trash*. She's my favorite kind of guest; unique, high energy, and contributing to the greater good. And her British accent is lovely, which is a bonus. We could have had a fine interview, the kind she had had many times before: "Wow! You picked up trash while you were paddleboarding! What was that like? Why did you want to paddleboard across the UK? How did you train," etc. All reasonable questions. But I looked at her Facebook, her website, and her previous interviews. I discovered she had been a single mom and had had an emotional breakdown in the "biscuit" aisle during a particularly tough patch of perimenopause. I knew my audience would appreciate that vivid detail. They could relate to being in a grocery store and having a little meltdown, being overwhelmed and hormonally off balance. The whole feel of the interview changed when I mentioned, "this whole journey started in the biscuit aisle of your grocery store." She chuckled and immediately relaxed, and we were connecting on a whole different level. She knew I had cared enough to learn about her, and we could have a genuine laugh together. Humor is a great connector. Getting background information and a feel for what motivates your guest will make for a memorable interview.

Once I schedule the interview, I send along a PDF with instructions to the guest (see Chapter 5), which includes a request for a brief introduction that I will read at the top of the show. On the day of the interview, I use what they send me and I edit it to make it cohesive and succinct. I've started paying more attention to writing an introduction that will appeal to my specific audience. I ask myself, "Would I want to listen to this? I talk about the relevance of the episode, especially if it is particularly timely, what I may have learned, and how it is important for the listener. I include how I became familiar with my guest's work if it adds some interest. One of my recent guests, Debby Waldman, had been a knitting buddy of mine in the mid-80's and a mutual friend reconnected us when my Debby's story about her relationship with her son was published in the New York Times. I'm challenging myself to add in a few personal details about how the subject connects with my life. As a podcaster interviewer, it's important to move away from a generic presence. People want to know you. As a therapist, I shy away from disclosing too much personal information; as a podcaster, I have begun adding tidbits about my relationship with the guest or the subject matter. It feels a little vulnerable to know that people from all over the world are listening to my story, but podcast interviewing is a full contact sport.

After I type up an introduction I'm happy with, I add some questions that are good starting points. I may jot down possible hashtags I want to remember when I publish the episode, which may be months from then. I have a yellow highlighter ready so when I'm speaking to my guest I can underscore important themes. I may come up with a good title as they are talking, as well as noting other guests who might be interested in the subject and I can tag on my social media.

Have the following handy before you start your interview: a glass of water, a clock, tissues, paper, and a pen. If you need a reminder to turn off the phone and turn on record, a sticky note works nicely. I keep my podcast introduction in a plastic sheet cover to avoid crinkle sounds when I'm reading it. I print out my guests' introductions, which I keep in a folder along with my other interview sheets. I also get permission to put the guests' names on my monthly newsletter email list, if I think it's appropriate, and confirm their correct email.

Interviewing can be nerve racking, especially when you first start out. When I interviewed Jean Kilbourne, the first researcher to talk about the link between advertising and eating disorders (my area of expertise), I was super nervous. I had seen her presentation 20 years ago and the groundbreaking documentary "Killing Us Softly" in graduate school. It left a deep impression. She may not be your idea of a rock star, but she was a real influencer in my career. Taking a few minutes to breathe into your belly (also called abdominal breathing) does wonders for nervous jitters. Your guest may be nervous too. Best if you are a little less nervous than they are.

It's important to be in a relaxed and open state of mind when interviewing. There's plenty of research on present moment awareness and mindfulness, and I encourage you to make those practices part of your preparation. Fully focusing on the conversation at hand will yield a better interview because you will be able to pick up subtle cues and follow themes that guide you to the next question. You'll be able to sense where the emotion is and follow those threads. You can't immerse yourself in the conversation if you are thinking about what you are going to eat for lunch. Do your best to stay present. For a great discussion of the benefits of mindfulness, check out my interview with "Mindful In May" founder Dr. Elise Biaylew.

Thorough preparation sets you up for a great interview. Your confidence will come through because you are not flying by the seat of your pants. You will come across as more calm and self-assured. The result will be a much better quality experience for both you and your audience.

CHAPTER 5
PREPARING YOUR GUEST

Your guest is busy. Preparing them well for the interview is respectful and professional. You want to make the experience of being on your podcast straightforward and simple, and you want to look professional. This will encourage trust because you've demonstrated you're a pro, not just a hobbyist with a mic. Your guests don't want to worry that they are going to embarrass themselves on a recorded interview that will be heard all over the world. My guests know I'm a psychotherapist, and I don't want them to worry that I'm going to try to psychoanalyze them for the world to hear. So I make my expectations very clear.

A couple of days before our scheduled interview, I sent them this PDF:

{Guest Person},

Thank you for being my guest on *Zestful Aging,* on {date here}, EST. Here are a couple of items to help you with preparation:
You will need to be on a computer, not a Smartphone.
You will need to be on **Google Chrome. This means Chrome must be your current browser. It's not enough to have just downloaded it.**
Please wear headphones.

You will get an email reminder from CAST 30 minutes before we start (please check your spam folder if you don't see it). We will chat first for a couple of minutes just to share some thoughts on the content before we record.

Once our interview is complete, it will be edited and put in the cue to upload. I will send you a direct link once it's dropped, which is always on a Saturday morning. I will share on my social media channels. I would love it if you shared too.

One important request: Because I am a psychotherapist with many years of treating eating disorders, I don't want to talk about weight loss diets.

Please send me a *short* intro (not bio) in the third person. This is just used for the purposes of introducing you, so please keep it concise.
Please contact me at <u>ZestfulAging@gmail.com</u> if you have any questions. You can also reach me on my cell.
Thank you so much for your time.

You'll notice that I have a clear request not to talk about weight loss diets. My day job is specializing in treating eating disorders so the last thing I want to talk about is dieting. If you have similar topics that are off limits, this is a good place to put them. Some hosts do not want to talk about politics or religion. It's best to be clear on this before the interview instead of running into an awkward situation or needing to edit it out. This is another example of setting clear expectations for your guest. It shows you are a seasoned pro, have dealt with many situations, and have things well in hand. And it further clarifies your mission. You might be surprised how relieved your guest is to know exactly what to expect.

Most people read these instructions and follow them, but some do not. I've received full page "intros" that guests suggest

I edit to suit my purposes. That's more work for me. And there may be other frustrations. One of my potential guests who had written several highly regarded books didn't know what a browser was, which is necessary to use my audio platform. I was really excited to interview her, but she simply could not figure out the tech. Try as I might, I wasn't able to connect. Sometimes things go wrong. Be prepared to lose interviews due to occasional tech problems. Once I was doing an interview with a major influencer and I noticed that the sky got very grey and lightning bolts were creating scary weather. I crossed my fingers that my internet didn't crash! I didn't think I'd get another chance to speak with her. It was so stressful that I had a hard time concentrating on what she was saying. Sometimes podcasting causes anxiety!

Assuming your goal is to have a substantive and memorable interview, building rapport and trust is a must. This is a skill that can be learned and executed in some straightforward and simple ways. As a therapist, I would never ask a client to open up immediately, not knowing me at all, and reveal themselves. It's much the same with a guest. They are often a little nervous, even if they've been interviewed many times. I recently had a guest who is the go-to expert in her field. She makes a living presenting to large audiences. She confided that she felt nervous before we started recording. I was happy to hear her relax as the interview went on.

Once my guest is connected with me via the internet, I start by making friendly small talk to help them feel comfortable. I ask them where they are located, and make pleasant, friendly chit chat to help them feel at ease. I tell them that my dog, Sparky, is right beside me (I'm always surprised at how many guests have their pets right beside them as well.) I might say, "It's just like we're having a coffee together in a cafe down the street." Sometimes I feel like a dentist saying, "This won't hurt a bit." I can often hear their relief when I say it will be informal and that I will take their lead. The basic message is it will be fun and there will be no surprises. I want to make them look good. This isn't "gotcha" journalism; it's a cooperative effort to inspire and entertain.

Then I go over exactly what they can expect during our talk. *I cannot emphasize the importance of this enough!* Preparing your guests helps them to feel comfortable, especially if they are new to being interviewed. You want your guests to feel comfortable so they can trust you. Otherwise, they will not open up and give you personal stories that have emotional content. And that's where the gold is. Remember: Emotional content is interesting. Soundbites are not. Laying the groundwork for how the interview will go helps them relax. I know that when I am guesting on someone else's podcast, I appreciate knowing their process beforehand. It makes it feel more professional and that my time is being respected. Don't make your guests wonder what to expect and have to ask questions such as, "Is this live or recorded? When will it go up?" Go through your process with them in an organized way. I have an actual list I read to them. I tell my guests that we podcast to almost a hundred countries, edit the episode, and take out any weird noises. I also give them an idea of the audience they are speaking to—"the NPR crowd, mostly women, about 28 through 55." This helps them tailor their comments to my specific audience, which adds to the quality of the interview.

I also like to say, "I'll start you out and take your lead." I often hear a sigh of relief. This response is especially true for my clients who know I am a psychotherapist. Nobody wants to feel like they are being psychoanalyzed—especially on a recorded interview! I explain that there will be five seconds of silence, I will introduce the show, and then I will welcome them. I used to use a pre-recorded introduction, but I decided I prefer it to sound more natural, with the little natural variations from week to week. I also think it is helpful that my guests hear the show's introduction. They hear what the audience hears and this gives them some context. It also gives them a couple more minutes to prepare themselves.

I always ask my guests to stay on the line after we say our good-byes and thank-yous. Why? I want to check on how it went for them. More often than not, they say, "This was really fun! You asked some great questions." You can put these kinds of comments and testimonials on your podcast website. But more importantly, they know I care about their experience. And showing you care builds greater trust. Several times I've spoken to my guest for more than an hour off-mic! I also stay in touch via social media, and I connect them with other guests they might enjoy. I see myself as a matchmaker of sorts, and it's been appreciated and reciprocated. It's a great way to build a far-reaching network. And it makes the whole experience richer for both you and your guest. So when you're feeling burned out on all of the logistics of producing your show, you will also remember how deeply satisfying it is.

By making these efforts, the podcast interview goes beyond the actual interview. I build relationships with my guests that can carry on in other ways. That's what makes podcasting so special. There are many guests across the world I would love to meet in person because our connection felt so great. In fact, the next time I travel to the UK, I have several people I plan on looking up! And one of my guests from the UK plans to come to the U.S. for Thanksgiving. We're making plans to meet. That's the beauty of connection.

Many podcasters use Skype or Zoom, and if that works for you that's fine. I've found Skype to be finicky, and neither Skype nor Zoom have great sound quality. I'm sensitive to sound, and I don't want to give listeners any reason to shut off the show. I've had good luck with CAST. The drawback is that you have to be using CHROME as a browser. Some of my guests are older and not tech savvy. Unless they have an assistant, they can have a tough time understanding the computer terminology. Think about what is most important to you and your audience, but be aware that having to endure poor sound can make even a great interview annoying.

Preparing your guests helps you come across like a pro. Your guests will appreciate your consideration and organization. They will feel that they are in good hands and are more likely to share emotional material because they feel confident in your abilities and, therefore, emotionally safe. Being intentional in the way you prepare your guests will help you stand out from the crowd.

CHAPTER 6
ANATOMY OF A GREAT INTERVIEW

The most important, and often most demanding, part of interviewing is deeply listening. Most of us think we are good listeners, but ask yourself this: When was the last time you had an uninterrupted, undistracted conversation for more than a few minutes? That kind of conversation has become so rare that a typical psychotherapy session can feel antiquated and a bit disorienting. In our distracted world, listening has become a thing of the past. It might be interesting to note how many times you feel heard and how many times you are giving your full attention while someone is speaking. Unfortunately, this trend of distraction has a real downside; most people say it's important for them to feel understood, but it's hard to understand another person's deep needs and fears when we are scrolling on our phones. Offering your guest your full attention will set you apart from other podcast hosts.

Listening also has a practical side. If you are truly listening, you will know what question to ask next. It will flow organically. Your guests will feel the quality of your attention and they will be more inclined to share personal stories with you. The conversation will feel special and take on more meaning when you are absolutely focused on what your guest is saying and expressing through their tone. There is something profound about being understood, and your guest will remember you for it. Your audience will wish you were interviewing them!

You want your guests to feel like they are the most important person in the world. It's your job to understand what motivates them and what brought them to this point. You want to get to know them as much as possible in the short time you have together. Your goal is to show them in the best light. The message you want to send is "I really care about you and what you do." It's easy to relax and open up when the person interviewing you is enthusiastic and admiring. If you don't feel that way, you might want to reconsider your choice of guests.

"Even, hovering attention" is a phrase I learned in graduate school while I was learning how to become a psychotherapist. It describes the delicately balanced stance necessary when you are interviewing both a client and a guest. You are paying attention to multiple things at the same time. In order to do this, you have to be in a calm and observant mindset. You can't be rattled, bored, or rushed. By the way, if you find yourself checking your Facebook (or knitting!) while your guests are talking, either they are boring or you are not being present. Neither bodes well for a good interview. "Even, hovering attention" is a state of mind that allows you to be open, flexible, and follow the evolving themes of the interview. Sometimes a conversation will take a totally unexpected turn. Be prepared to shift gears and follow your guest if you think it will be interesting to your audience. Spontaneous tangents can make for a captivating interview. It's a balance, though. Too much of a tangent can create an unwieldy interview which doesn't feel coherent.

Your questions should have purpose and direction: Are you trying to have them explain their work, a difficult time in their lives, or how they made a particular decision? These are split-second decisions, and they are based on what you think will most interest your audience. You only have a finite amount of time, and some good material will be left on the "cutting room floor." But it's better to leave your audience wanting more than boring them.

Obviously, if you ask a close-ended question, you will get a closed-ended answer. I like to start with a question the guest has provided, and go from there. I think this also builds goodwill because I let my guests have some control of how the interview will flow. When I was training to be a psychotherapist, one of my clinical supervisors said something that has influenced me as a podcast interviewer: "The devil is always found in the details." Ask the follow-up questions. Here are some of my favorite follow-ups: "In what way?" "How so?" and "Can you say more about that?" Those questions tend to produce more spontaneous and interesting material. Don't be satisfied with rote answers. Dig deeper. Let your curiosity lead. This will help you connect more deeply with your guests and set you apart from other hosts.

Curiosity is one of the best qualities for an interviewer. You'll never have to fake it if you are speaking with someone about whom you are curious. A sincere interest in another person comes across as enthusiastic, and that feeling is contagious. I am smiling when I introduce my podcast, and that comes through in the sound of my voice. My excitement and eagerness to speak with my guest captures my audience's interest and has a positive effect on my guest. They can't help but match my energy.

Keep in mind that everything is for the benefit of your audience. You may want to hear more about an obscure aspect of their lives, but ask yourself if your audience will be interested. Using that as the guiding principle will serve you well. When I listen to other interviewers, I notice they often change topics too soon for my taste. They leave the money on the table! Follow up questions can yield juicy details that go beyond the original, often rehearsed, answer. Try drawing out your guest by asking them to give more details or by giving them a moment of silence to say more. Slow down and let the conversation evolve naturally rather than asking rapid-fire questions. We're not gathering data. We're sharing an emotional connection with our audience.

When I first began my Podcast, my goal was to get the most information from my guest. It was as if I was in therapist mode conducting an evaluation. It felt a little like work. My interviews ran upwards of an hour. I was just so happy that I had a guest agree to be on the show! An hour works really well for some shows, but for me the last fifteen minutes lost steam. With practice, you will develop a sense of how long is just right. I've been tempted too many times to ask one more question because I'm really interested in the subject matter. But when the conversation has a nice flow and is wrapping up in a logical place, it's best not to extend it. You can always have the guest on for another interview if you think they are that compelling. Generally speaking, better it be too short than too long. I've found 30 minutes is the sweet spot for my show, and it's roughly the time of the average American commute—a time when many people tune in.

It's important to think about each episode in terms of a beginning, a middle, and an end. Each episode should be a complete story in itself. In the beginning, your audience learns about your guests and why you've chosen them as guests. Who are they? Why are they special? Where does their story begin? Then we talk about particular challenges they've overcome or surprises they've encountered. The end is mostly focused on what they learned, how they've changed, and what they want to share with the audience. I usually ask for tips or guidance that they can share with my listeners, and they often give some great advice. An interesting story is fun, but it's more important to offer your audience some guidance if possible. Learning something as a result of that episode will be more valuable to them. Giving your listeners something concrete to do is sometimes referred to as "actionable steps" and most content creators recommend this technique as a way to engage your audience.

I recently interviewed Barbara Mancini, a nurse who was arrested for allegedly giving her dying father a lethal dose of morphine and aiding an attempted suicide. She spent a year fighting her case in court. She had very specific recommendations for our audience about researching each specific Hospice agency before hiring them, and understanding the political and religious environment in which your loved one is living. Her father lived in a politically conservative town in Pennsylvania, which had a great impact on how his advanced directives were considered. She gave my audience relevant and helpful advice about how to choose a Hospice service for one's loved one.

Your mood comes through when you are interviewing a guest. A couple of times, I had a hard time hearing a guest and we were both quite frustrated. By the time we figured out the problem we were both a little grouchy and I think it affected the tone of the interview. We had both used up our cheerfulness and anticipation, and it felt more like a task. I've heard that some hosts put themselves in a happy mood by singing before they go live. Experiment with what works for you. I take some deep breaths and remind myself how much I love the opportunity to talk to people about their projects.

When I first started as a psychotherapist and as a podcaster, I had a list of questions I knew I wanted to ask during an interview. I had an evaluation form I printed up for my clients, complete with spaces to write their answers. I was afraid I would forget to ask important questions. I relied on that sheet. I would have felt lost without it! When you are still a beginner, have three or four questions ready to ask. After a while, you may only need one or two questions to get things rolling. You'll have more confidence and you'll be able to pick out what will be most interesting to your audience right from the first answer. In that way, you will tailor your conversation to your listeners, not just the general public. Listen for where the emotion is. Is their voice cracking? Has their tone changed? Tune into the feeling of the conversation. What are they emphasizing? Are they repeating themes? This is where the gold lies. Using your intuition as your guide can be a great help. This is how you can go deeper than just asking the obvious questions.

If your guest is obviously emotionally upset, it's important to be respectful. You might ask, "Would you be willing to talk more about that?" They will appreciate your consideration, and most likely continue. My husband likes to tease me by asking if I made my guest cry. I don't set out to do that, but I do pride myself in asking questions that give them an opportunity to share deeper feelings. Also, don't be afraid to pause before you speak again. Give them a chance to say more. Sometimes they will continue and give you the best material when you least expect it.

As a podcast interviewer, you are juggling several things at the same time. You are focusing on the moment, filing away information you want to return to, and anticipating the next question. You are assessing whether to let the guest continue speaking on the same subject or shift gears. Do you add anything or just listen? Be quiet, or say "hmm" to let them know you are listening? It requires serious multi-tasking and takes full focus and concentration. You cannot be distracted. There's an interviewing "zone" and it takes energy. I avoid interviewing two guests in one day. Some hosts like to "batch record" because it can be more efficient. That would not work for me, but you might try it to see if you can sustain your energy and interest over several interviews.

The interview is not about getting the most information possible. Think of it more like an experience you and your guest are sharing with your audience. Ideally, you want your listener to wish that they could participate in the conversation. Gathering information is fine, but you want to offer more than interesting facts; you want to offer a feeling of resonance. If the listeners' emotions have not been engaged, the episode will not be memorable to them. It will be lost among all of the other information and factoids they are bombarded with daily. One of my guests bemoaned the fact that we ran out of time before she could tell more stories. But the one story she told was powerful and memorable; it's a game of quality over quantity.

CHAPTER 7
FINDING YOUR VOICE

Many of us don't give much thought to our speaking voices. Except when we're recording the outgoing message on our phones—then we may cringe. We think we're stuck with the voice that we have. We do not put much emphasis on the actual sound of our voice as it relates to podcast interviewing. That's a mistake. As a podcaster who is primarily audio-only, my voice is the only tool I have to connect with my listeners. And if it's unpleasant, it doesn't matter how interesting the interview.

According to celebrity voice coach Roger Love, the voice is an instrument that can be tuned. He's helped many actor celebrities change their voices for roles they are playing, and he's made quite a business of it. Among his Grammy winners are Bradley Cooper for the film *A Star is Born*. There are many simple and practical techniques to improve your podcasting voice. You might be surprised that the first thing Love advises is to breathe through your nose. That simple step helps keep your vocal cords stay moist. He suggests that after a period we should close our lips and take a breath. It might seem unnatural at first, but it ensures the vocal cords stay lubricated and your voice holds out. If you are "batch recording"—recording more than one podcast at a time—you will notice your voice gets strained and weaker the more you talk. Listening to a strained voice is unpleasant. And it's easy to avoid.

Roger Love notes that 80% of people speak in a monotone, which is boring and uninspiring. If you want to capture your audience's attention, you must vary your tone. Adding melody and volume, according to Love, is vitally important. Both impart emotion, which brings your listeners closer. He goes so far as to say that your listeners are more tuned into the *sounds* you are making than the actual words. Sounds have direct emotional impact, and paying attention to your intonations will make a world of difference. It's well worth your time to consider the impact of how you sound.

Voice actor and podcaster Jodi Krangle points out that we use different tones of voice depending on to whom we are talking. We don't sound the same with our family, our friends, and our podcast audience. She recommends using the appropriate tone when you are speaking with your audience, based on who they are. Your voice should sound different if your audience are business people than if they are remote control airplane enthusiasts. Think in terms of having a dialogue with them. It's helpful to imagine your audience being right there as you record. This gets to the importance of knowing your audience, which is one of the basic rules of podcasting. Gather as much data as you can about who is actually listening. Studying your analytics can be extremely helpful. I was surprised to find that there are people listening to *Zestful Aging* who are in their 20's! A Facebook group connected to the podcast is a good way to speak with your audience directly and poll them about things that are important to them.

On a practical note, Krangle also suggests making sure you are hydrated. Fluids take about 20 minutes for your body to absorb, so plan ahead. If you are suffering from a cold or allergies, Nashville vocal coach Judy Rodman recommends a voice actors' secret elixir: mixing one part pineapple juice and four parts water. This mixture helps the vocal folds absorb moisture. Pineapples have bromelain, an enzyme with anti-inflammatory properties and research shows that it's great for clearing out mucus.

Both Love and Krangle recommend a voice warm up. Love prescribes practicing scales, and Krangle suggests singing—even if you can't hold a tune. It gets your cords warm and flexible, and puts you in a good mood. Choose a song that's uplifting and fun. Tuning your voice to be emotionally engaging will put you in an elevated class of interviewers.

In terms of finding and using your figurative voice, you will need to make some decisions about your podcast's mission and clarify what associations will benefit you. Because as a quality podcaster, you will be sought after by advertisers. Advertisers are beginning to see the enormous benefits of sponsoring podcasts, although experts say that we're still in the early stages of ad spending. According to Advertisecast, podcast advertisements are five times as effective as web ads. Podcasts are the perfect medium for advertisers—the work of finding the company's ideal customers has already been done for them. Instead of casting a wide net and advertising to the general public, they have access to a curated audience who is much more likely to buy their product. Podcast listeners are loyal and trust their hosts, so listeners are more apt to buy what is advertised on their favorite podcast. Industry experts predict podcasts will become much more important in advertising in the near future because the format is more effective at reaching potential customers. One reason for this is podcasts have fewer ads per hour than radio or TV. This means that the advertising message doesn't get lost in a set of commercials. Furthermore, podcast ads feel fresh and original, rather than boring and repetitive like pre-recorded radio commercials. They also blend better into the content of the episode, especially if they are read by the trusted host. The best podcast ads are voiced live by hosts, in their own words, so it feels like more of a personal recommendation. This makes ads well integrated into shows, keeping listeners engaged. I've been very careful to advertise for companies whose products I've sampled and can honestly endorse. Since the ad is a reflection of my Podcast, and ultimately of me, it's important to choose wisely.

As you hone your skills, you will have more choice of potential products to advertise. It's exciting to be sought after. You might have to ask yourself questions that you hadn't planned on considering; Do you want to advertise for hair dye? (I don't) Other podcasts? Services you would never use? I've enjoyed advertising for some sports products that I use and would benefit my listeners. I like being associated with these products because they are good quality and further my message of aging zestfully. I'm putting out a congruent message—not just adding random sponsorships to earn a few bucks. I want every decision to be intentional, so I can keep the quality of my production high. In that way, my audience feels I respect and care for them. They don't want to be treated as mere customers. This maintains the integrity of your work and keeps your podcast different from radio and even other podcasts.

Since I've been podcasting, I've been fascinated by listening to other interviewers. Now that you are working on your interview skills, you will notice what other people do well—and don't do so well. I was surprised to discover Oprah tends to talk over her guests! That's a bad habit I also have that I've been trying hard to break. I found that Jerry Seinfeld, on his Netflix interview show "Comedians in Cars Getting Coffee," has a disarming way of asking his guests questions and often gets rich material. David Letterman seems to talk about himself and his son. Terry Gross on NPR's *Fresh Air* asks difficult questions and sounds quite curious and engaged. Perhaps that is why she has such a following.

It's not difficult to find podcast hosts who seem to love the sound of their own voices. Talking about oneself is a slippery slope. Talking about yourself too much can make you appear to be a novice rather than a seasoned host. Make sure there's a good reason for you to tell your story—does it add anything? Or is it just fun to hear yourself talk? Go back to the idea of being intentional. My default is to keep it about my guest unless I have a good reason to share my own story. Is it relevant? Does it make a good point? Does it further the conversation? It may serve to help your audience get to know you a bit better. But just share with some forethought. Again, it's about your audience. If you think they will appreciate it, that's your best guide. As you gain more experience and confidence, you will develop your own style. Your audience will come to expect your particular way of interviewing.

It's important to know if your audience is resonating with your style. Make sure you have a way for your listeners to give you feedback on your show. A website devoted to your podcast with an easy way to leave comments is helpful in getting input from your listeners. It helps to know what episodes they related to most. I mention that I love to hear from my listeners right in the introduction of every episode. It brings the listeners in and helps them feel like they are part of a community. Sometimes podcasting can feel like you are in a vacuum. It's validating to receive comments from a bona fide listener. You can look at your analytics, but we don't always know if the person was listening—just that they downloaded the episode. Again, people crave being part of a community, especially in these times of intense disconnection. Offer them a place to feel known and understood. You are like a reliable friend who shares similar interests.

CHAPTER 8
HAVING FUN

One of the comments I get most, and that I'm most proud of, is that my guests have fun. In fact, they often seem surprised at how much fun they have. My own enjoyment must be contagious. There's something thrilling about speaking with someone you admire and asking them questions that truly matter to you. This thrill is intensified when they are in another time zone or culture. You know your voice is being heard beyond your own little world. Or when you are talking about your guest's book that isn't even available for purchase yet. It's fun to feel special!

Speaking to someone thousands of miles away over the computer still seems like magic to me. This was the case when I interviewed Adam Minter, the author of "Junkyard Planet" and "Secondhand." As a serious thrift shopper, I had some worries that my purchases took away items from people who were truly needy. One of my close friends admonished me for buying up clothes that were meant for people who couldn't afford to shop retail. I was able to ask him about this directly. What a privilege to be able to get his perspective—he's arguably the world's expert on thrifting! Now I can be "thrift proud", which is a slogan I saw recently on Facebook.

Judy Woodruff of PBS is one of my favorite newscasters. I watch her almost every night, deeply admiring her poise and professional demeanor. And I notice that she stumbles over words and has to correct herself. Seeing her do this helps me feel less pressure to be flawless. Voice actress Jodi Krangle quips that she says, "you know" far too often. Some of these fillers can be edited out, but don't get too hung up on sounding perfect. Our audience wants to hear our humanness. They want to relate to us. Sounding like a regular person is part of the charm of being a podcast host. Better to be exuberant and stumble over some words than come across like an autotron.

Having fun with your podcast is also important if you are going to avoid podfade. Think about the parts that make it most fun for you. How do you express your personality? What are your trademark questions? Expressing yourself feels good and lets your listeners know you more. Being creative is good for our mental health. I usually ask my guests what their legacy will be. It's a big question, and I enjoy hearing guests wrestle with it. Look for ways to make producing your podcast the most fun it can be. My dog is always right beside me during recording, so I decided to add that into the intro. Even when the subject matter is serious, try to keep things in perspective. Enjoying the process will go a long way towards preventing burnout. I make a habit of finding some levity in the subject matter, even if it's serious. Sharing a laugh with a guest makes it more fun for both of us.

Playing your own interviews back can be fun too. It's a good practice to see if there are areas that could use improvement. It has its painful aspects, though. I have a terrible habit of asking questions that are way too long. One time one of my clients asked, "Was that a question?" I'm working on it. Overall, I'm pleased with the kinds of questions I ask. Once, after listening to one of my interviews, I found myself commenting out loud, "that's a really good question!" For a moment, I forgot it was me who was doing the asking.

There's so much work involved in producing a podcast; if you are not enjoying it, you will soon give it up. Be flexible enough to experiment with changing things that aren't working. Over the years, I've become more comfortable allowing my personality to show through and discuss sensitive topics, or even embarrassing moments. My earlier interviews sound more formal and tentative. I've enjoyed pushing myself out of my comfort zone and revealing more of myself. Ultimately, your audience is looking to be entertained, even if they are also being informed. And we're all looking for a bit of relief from the pressures of life. Making a point to have some fun will be appreciated by your guest and your audience.

CHAPTER 9
THE TAKEAWAY

Here are the major points we've covered in the previous chapters. It might be helpful to keep this page handy in your recording area.

- Deep listening is crucial

- Curiosity and enthusiasm go a long way

- Ask follow up questions

- Vary the tone and volume of your voice

- Your audience is always first

- Allow your unique personality to shine through

- Anticipate that each episode will take several hours to produce

- Only invite guests who interest you

- Enjoy yourself

Hosting my Podcast has enriched my life in ways that are hard for even me to describe. It's made me smarter, better read, and more interesting. I also feel more hopeful because I am meeting people all over the world contributing to the common good. I've also realized that even though my guests may have published acclaimed books or are sought-after influencers, we're all just people. Maybe that's why I'm able to contact culture-changers and invite them to be on my show. As one of my friend's quips, "We're all just bozos on the same bus."

My wish for you is that you also feel a deep sense of satisfaction from speaking with fascinating people you wouldn't have an opportunity to meet face to face. Especially in these difficult times, connecting with others is the antidote to despair. Best of luck in your podcasting adventure, and maybe we'll meet at a podcasting conference in the future. Please introduce yourself!

Feel free to contact me at ZestfulAging@gmail.com to share your interview experiences and offer feedback.

NICOLE CHRISTINA is the host of the acclaimed Zestful Aging Podcast, an interview show heard in 98 countries. She's also a psychotherapist of 30 years, specializing in eating disorders. Nicole's guests are change makers from a variety of disciplines; filmmakers, writers, advocates, poets, musicians, scientists, athletes and entrepreneurs, many of whom are top experts in their fields. The Show has a humanitarian focus, and looks at the importance of leaving your own legacy. Leaving a legacy is a way of contributing to the common good, which has shown to have a significant impact on aging well. Zestful Aging is a media partner with the International Federation of Ageing, based in Toronto. Nicole is the author of: "Not Just Chatting; How to Become a Master Podcast Interviewer".

Find out more at ZestfulAging.com.

- https://www.linkedin.com/in/nicolechristinalcsw/
- http://NicoleChristina.com
- http://Facebook.com/ZestfulAging
- @ZestfulAging.https://www.linkedin.com/in/nicolechristinalcsw
- https://instagram.com/zestfulaging/
- https://www.pinterest.com/ZestfulAging/

www.ingramcontent.com/pod-product-compliance
Lightning Source LLC
Chambersburg PA
CBHW061602220326
41597CB00053B/2815